I0622577

How to Live a

Happy

Life

7 Keys to
Get You Started

Miriam Jones

REALLY**EDUCATED**

This book is not intended to provide personalized legal, accounting, financial, mental or emotional health, therapy or investment advice. Readers are encouraged to seek the counsel of competent professionals regarding such matters as interpretation of the law, proper accounting procedures, financial planning, mental health counseling, personal therapy, and investment strategies. The Author and Publisher specifically disclaim any liability, loss, or risk which is incurred as a consequence, directly or indirectly, of the use and application of any of the contents of this work.

DEDICATION

This book is dedicated to everyone doing their best to live the life of their dreams. It is for the ones who struggle on a daily basis to keep everything together yet still find a way to make things happen.

This is for the dreamers, the lovers, the achievers, the believers. This book is for you. All of you. I hope that this piece inspires you in your journey to live a happy life. It is a process, but it is not impossible. The most exciting part is that you can start today! You do not have to wait for things to change to be happy. Happiness exists now. It is your choice.

So, I encourage you to be bold, and take the steps necessary to get where you want to be. You can live the life you have always wanted. Every success begins in your mind. I believe in you and wish you all the best.

Live Life. Be Happy. Dream Big.

CONTENTS

PART THREE

Your Actions

18

PART FOUR

Your Mindset

25

"What Do I Do Now?"

29

"What is Happiness to You, and Who in the World is Miriam Jones?"

Everyone wants to be happy right? Some find joy in time spent with family, recreation, work, time alone, or reading a good book. Others may think happiness comes from religion or finding peace within. Many more seek happiness in money and material possessions, big houses, and fancy cars.

What is happiness to you? Take a moment to reflect on that. If you had to define happiness, what would you say it is?

Write your answer on a sheet of paper.

Now pause for a moment. What if I told you that you could have the life you want starting today? Would you believe me? Probably not (that is unless you are already living it, and if that is true congratulations). It's highly unlikely you'd still be reading if that were the case. But if it is, you can stop reading now.

I want to speak to those people who feel like they deserve more but just do not know how to get it. The people who are truly hungry for change. The people who desperately just need a little guidance to get from where they are now to where they want to be.

Of course, I am not going to promise you a perfect life, I can't even guarantee what I am about to tell you will work for you. But, if you would believe just for a moment that the dream you have in your heart is possible, I will share with you what I've learned that has changed my life and that I know could change yours too.

So, who exactly am I? That's a great question. At the moment that I am writing this I am following my own dream. I have been given a gift to encourage others to achieve their highest potential. I enjoy learning and sharing and truly get excited when I see others succeed. Beyond that, I grew up in a small town where my father was a civilian in the Air Force and my mother worked in a factory. I spent a lot of time alone during childhood and didn't have many friends.

When I got to middle school, things changed for me. I discovered that I had a knack for running which later opened the opportunity for me to attend college on a full athletic scholarship. I've worked for many of the nation's top companies doing everything from vacation sales and cleaning toilets, to academic advising for a global educational services corporation. Fast forward, I went to law school, passed the bar on my first try, managed a law firm, went back to school, became a graphic designer, and even a licensed real estate agent.

Despite all my success, I still found myself feeling unfulfilled, spinning my wheels to get out of debt, and facing one failed relationship after the next. Until one day I finally had enough. I decided I did not want to live that way anymore. Something had to change. And here I am today. I took a chance on myself and made a decision. I applaud you for doing the same. Your choice to read this book shows that you are dedicated to finding happiness and a better life. It is my pleasure to guide you on this journey.

What to Expect

This book is formatted to make it as easy as possible for you to get started on the road to better. Each chapter provides a brief description of a concept and some practical applications and affirmations for you to recite. As you do, you will find day by day your motivation will grow and your ability to put it all into action will increase. So, let's get started.

PART ONE

Your Passions

Discovering What You Love and Going After It

Key #1 Find Your Passion

What do you love? What are you good at?

From childhood we are told to go to school, get a good job, save and this will provide security and happiness. I'm not sure about you, but for me that formula did not work. I went to school, I got many "good" jobs, and still found myself with tons of student loan debt and wishing I had more time to do the things that I enjoyed. This disappointment was the result of doing things that I thought would lead to success, rather than going after what I was truly passionate about.

Finding your passion is important because it will drive you. There is a natural inclination to focus on, nurture, and celebrate the things you love.

For example, take a moment to think about the important people in your life. Do you run away from them, or do you look forward to spending time with them? Do you feel miserable around them, or do you feel comfortable and excited to see them? Do you feel like it is a waste of time to engage with them, or does time not matter when they are around?

You see, doing the things you love will always flow naturally for you. This is so important. If you can find your real passion and do what you love, you will not only enjoy it, but you will also be committed to it, find fulfillment in it, and most importantly it will be rewarding for you.

HAPPINESS PRINCIPLE:

If you can find your real passion and do what you love, you will not only enjoy it, but you will also be committed to it, find fulfillment in it, and most importantly it will be rewarding for you.

DECLARATIONS: Look in the mirror and say… *"I am committed to doing what I love!"*, *"I will follow my heart!"* Touch your heart and say… *"I have a happy life!"*

HAPPINESS ACTION PLAN

1. Every time you catch yourself debating whether a decision or action is right for

you or you are feeling pressured to do something to please someone else, place your hand on your heart and say, "I will follow my heart." This will act as a reminder to be true to yourself first. After a while, following your instincts will become second nature.

2. At the end of each day write down one way that you decided to follow your passion and one way that you failed to do so. Take time to reflect on the outcome of each decision. This time will allow you to become more aware of your actions and see which decisions support your happiness journey and which ones do not.

Key #2 Go for It!

Now that you have found your passion it's time to take off. Ok, ok, I know you're thinking hey, I haven't done any research, I don't know where to begin and I don't have the money to start! I get it. Trust me, this is probably the hardest part of the process especially for overthinkers or those of us who need to have things all planned out first.

Although it is very important to have some knowledge and understanding of the area you would like to pursue, all too often we let the details get in the way of making progress or as one of my mentors would call it "analysis paralysis." This is something that you definitely do not want.

Take it in baby steps if you have to. The idea is just to start somewhere. The key is to do something every single day that contributes to your ultimate goal. It is the culmination of these small steps that will make you a master at your craft, build your confidence, and ultimately your reputation. Greatness is built through repetition. A little effort over time leads to big results in the long run.

HAPPINESS PRINCIPLE:

Greatness is built through repetition. A little effort over time leads to big results in the long run.

By making the decision to get moving, you can find out much quicker what works and what doesn't.

Let's say you spend months thinking about, researching, and crafting the perfect plan. Then, you put it into action and guess what? It's a complete flop. Of course, you will still learn from it, but you will not get that time back.

Now imagine if you just took the same idea and went with it and found out right away that it wasn't so great after all? Learning through failure is crucial in making progress and ultimately achieving growth and success. So, take the leap and get started. You will thank me later.

DECLARATIONS: Look in the mirror and say…*"I will take action and not overthink!"* Touch your heart and say…*"I have a happy life!"*

HAPPINESS ACTION PLAN

1. Write down two goals that you would like to accomplish in the next three months that align with your passion.

2. Call one of your close friends and tell them about your goals. This will help to create the accountability and support often needed when things get difficult.

PART TWO

Your Beliefs

Embracing the Power That Exists Beyond You

Key #3 Have Faith

We have all heard that faith can move mountains. Indeed, there is power in believing in something bigger than you. It's crucially important in your journey to happiness that you be able to rely on something outside of yourself.

When difficulties come and illogical things happen if you do not have faith, you can become easily discouraged. Faith involves believing that despite whatever happens, there is a purpose and there is hope.

HAPPINESS PRINCIPLE:

Faith involves believing
that despite whatever
happens, there is a
purpose and there is hope.

Without getting into a discussion on religion, the reason having faith is so important is that without it, you are limited to your own strength. Faith opens your mind to take the pressure off your limitations and allows you to truly live in freedom.

The mind is a powerful thing. We are incredible creatures. Total health (mental, spiritual, physical, and emotional) is vital to achieving our highest self. How you align yourself each day is up to you. Whether it is through prayer, quiet meditation, visualization or simply embracing positivity and gratitude, having faith and believing is a must.

DECLARATIONS: Look in the mirror and say…*"I believe I am here for a reason!"*, *"I believe my life has meaning!"*, *"I believe I can achieve my goals!"*, *"I believe there is hope for my situation!"* Touch your heart and say…*"I have a happy life!"*

HAPPINESS ACTION PLAN

1. Make a list of the areas in your life that you struggle with. Take some time to review the list and release your attempts to control those situations.

2. Do something today that you have been afraid to try. After you have done it, take note of how you feel. The more you take the opportunity to step outside of your comfort zone, the more you will realize many of your fears are truly unfounded.

Key #4 Don't Force Anything

If you have made it this far, congratulations on your journey. You have taken the first steps to achieving a happy life. As you move forward, undoubtedly you will run into a few challenges and when you do, there is something that you always need to remember: **NEVER FORCE ANYTHING!** That's right. If it is not working, there is a reason. What is meant to happen will happen when it is supposed to happen.

HAPPINESS
PRINCIPLE:

What is meant to happen will happen when it is supposed to happen.

This was something that I struggled with for quite some time until I learned to relax and let go. If there was a task that needed to be done and I just couldn't get it right, I would keep trying and trying and trying ultimately leading to stress and frustration. I've had plenty of angry moments and wasted energy blaming everything under the sun and even above the earth for that matter.

When I finally learned how to let go and simply move on to something else, I found time and time again the very thing that was giving me so much difficulty was solved with little effort down the road. The wisdom of being able to pivot and focus energy in a productive direction rather than wasting time on negativity is key to maintaining internal peace and emotional well-being.

Are there areas in your life that don't seem to be working out? What is it that you are trying to make happen or force into reality? Is it a relationship? A promotion? A business idea? Whatever it is, I challenge you to take a step back, breathe, and refocus your energy towards the areas in your life that are working. Soon you will find by simply working with the flow instead of against it, the doors that you have been trying to force open with your own efforts will either begin to open on their own or new opportunities will come your way. Choose to live in the flow.

DECLARATIONS: Look in the mirror and say…*"What is meant for me is for me, what is not, is not!"* Touch your heart and say…*"I have a happy life!"*

HAPPINESS ACTION PLAN

1. Choose to focus on the areas of your life that are successful.

2. Try the 3 strikes method the next time you face a challenge with something. Give it your best shot 3 times, if it does not work let it go and move onto something else.

PART THREE

Your Actions

Living Responsibly and Engaging Consciously

Key #5 Money Matters

Now comes the fun part. Let's talk about money. We all know the saying "money can't buy happiness", which in a way can be true. While happiness does come from within, money can help with your overall wellness by reducing the stress of having to worry about your material needs being met.

Money is a tool. The more responsibly you learn to use it, the more opportunity you will have to engage in fulfilling experiences.

HAPPINESS

PRINCIPLE:

Money is a tool. The
more responsibly you
learn to use it, the more
opportunity you will have
to engage in fulfilling
experiences.

I am sure you have been through tough times
like going to buy food and purchasing the
cheapest product you can find instead of getting
what you really want, having your child ask for
something and not being able to get it for them
because money is tight, or having to borrow from
a friend or relative to put gas in your car just to
get to work.

If any of this sounds familiar, I want you to
take a moment and imagine a life where you are
not forced to pinch pennies or constantly worry

about the price of things. Imagine being able to really get the things that you want without settling for something less. Imagine not having to worry about how bills are going to get paid each month. This is a life of freedom, this is a life of security, and all this is possible when you appreciate and understand the concept that money matters. Sometimes the thing that holds us back from receiving what we truly desire is our perspective.

When you view money in a positive light with the understanding of the doors it can open and the pressure it can relieve, money is no longer the enemy. Instead, you embrace the fact that you have been given the assignment to manage it in such a way that would enrich your life and the lives of those around you.

DECLARATIONS: Look in the mirror and say… *"Money is important!"*, *"I will manage my money responsibly."*, *"I will use my money not only to improve my life, but to impact the lives of* *those around me."* Touch your heart and say… *"I have a happy life!"*

HAPPINESS ACTION PLAN

1. Think about what you have been taught about money. Do you currently have limiting beliefs that keep you from achieving your financial goals?

2. Write down 3 financial goals that you would like to accomplish this year.

3. What are four areas of your finances that you would like to improve? (increase income, decrease debt, increase savings etc.)

Bonus: Go to www.reallyeducated.com to receive your free Financial Goals Worksheet.

Key #6 Learn to Listen

There is great power that comes with the ability to listen. As humans, our default is to want to be heard. Most of the time when the opportunity presents itself, we dive right into telling our story or expressing our feelings. Every word that comes out of a person's mouth reflects their inner thoughts and character. Therefore, if you are to make true connections with those around you, it is important to be able to listen first.

HAPPINESS PRINCIPLE:

If you are to make true connections with those around you, it is important to be able to listen first.

Have you ever met someone and asked how they were doing, just to be polite only to find that they have a whole life story to share about what's been going on with them? I often have strangers walk up to me and just start talking. Randomly revealing parts of their lives that I would not have guessed or imagined asking about. Each time, I am reminded of how important it is for us to engage with others on a regular basis.

When you learn to listen instead of always sharing, you can foster better relationships, become more trustworthy, and an overall better judge of your surroundings.

People will always reveal their true selves over time. There isn't really a need to dig if you just listen and observe. Being able to do so will save you a lot of headache in the long run. Give it a try, instead of being the one sharing all the time try to listen more. You might be surprised at the results.

DECLARATIONS: Look in the mirror and say…*"I will listen first!"* Touch your heart and say…*"I have a happy life!"*

HAPPINESS ACTION PLAN

1. In your next conversation make it a point to ask the other person a few questions and practice listening to what they have to say instead of sharing.

2. Reflect on ways that you can become a better listener.

PART FOUR

Your Mindset

Choosing to Be Happy

Key #7 Stop Doing Things That Make You Unhappy

Congratulations! You have made it to the final step. Along the way you have learned how to find your passion, go after your dreams, walk by faith, allow things to happen naturally, the importance of money, and how to develop better listening skills. The final rule I have for you is a simple one: If you want to be happy, stop doing things that make you unhappy. You read that correctly. It really is that straightforward.

Happiness exists internally and involves making choices. When you choose not to entertain thoughts that disrupt your spirit, your actions will create an environment that nurtures contentment. Each person is equipped with an internal value system that defines what happiness is. If you do things that align with your value system, you will be happy.

If there were one word I could use to describe how to determine whether something is in alignment, it would be peace. Do the things that bring you peace.

HAPPINESS PRINCIPLE:

Do the things that bring you peace.

If a situation constantly brings you anxiety, stress, worry, or doubt it is likely not for you at that time. Trust your instincts. You never want to fight yourself. Your thoughts and feelings are valid. They exist to help you survive. The more you try to fight them, the more you will struggle. It takes some getting used to, but once you learn to make the conscious decision to be content in any situation, you will find true peace and happiness.

DECLARATIONS: Look in the mirror and say…*"I choose to be happy!", "I choose to do things that bring me peace!"*, *"I choose not to entertain thoughts that disrupt my spirit."* Touch your heart and say…*"I have a happy life!"*

HAPPINESS ACTION PLAN

1. Make a list of 5 things that bring you peace. Focus on setting aside time each day to do at least one of those things.

2. Make a list of 5 things that you are grateful for. Each morning recite your list out loud. This will help you to get your day started in a positive way.

3. Each time a negative thought enters your mind, simply say "thank you, but no

thank you." Doing this will help you to stop entertaining thoughts that are unproductive.

"What Do I Do Now?"

You made it! You are now well on your way towards a life you love, a life that is filled with peace, fulfillment and happiness.

There are two things that I want you to take away from this book:

1. Happiness is a daily choice.
2. Living your dream is completely possible.

Never stop learning and always be true to your heart. When you approach life with a positive mindset, obstacles that come up cannot destroy the joy you carry on the inside. Life is full of challenges and sometimes things do not work out the way we want them to, however, it is still completely possible to be happy in the midst of it all. Remember, happiness is a gift that exists inside of you. Once you learn to embrace, nourish, and recognize it, you become unstoppable.

I invite you to visit www.reallyeducated.com to receive these special free resources:

1. Daily Happiness Declarations Printout
2. Financial Goals Worksheet
3. Happiness Action Plan

SHARE THE HAPPINESS

"The more you learn to share, the brighter your world will become."

-Miriam Jones

The greatest gift you can give is the gift of knowledge. If you found this book to be helpful, I ask you to share it with someone in your life. We are here not only to live to our fullest potential, but to help others along the way. Indeed, the more that you align with the people around you the more harmonious your life will become. As you sow into others you will begin to see a harvest of joy surrounding you.

I challenge you, as you continue your life journey, to share what you have learned each time you have the opportunity. Remember where you started from and the reason you read this book. There is someone out there just like you who is searching for the same answers that you were.

At the end of the day always remember to **Live Life, Be Happy and Dream Big!**

Your best is yet to come!

INDEX